DINOSAURS

Illustrated by
Georgene Griffin

Cover illustration of *Tyrannosaurus rex* by
Howard S. Friedman

Copyright © 2006 Kidsbooks LLC
www.kidsbooks.com

Manufactured in China

0306-2C

Visit us at www.kidsbooks.com

INTRODUCTION

This book will teach you how to draw many different types of dinosaurs. Some are more difficult to draw than others, but if you follow along, step by step, then (most important!) practice on your own, you'll soon be able to draw all the dinosaurs in this book. You also will learn the methods for drawing anything you want by breaking it down into basic shapes.

The most basic and commonly used shape is the oval. There are many variations of ovals: some are small and round, others are long and narrow, many are in between.

Most of the figures in this book begin with some kind of oval. Then other shapes and lines are added to to it to form the basic dinosaur outline.

Most times, a free-form oval is used, like the ones pictured below. In addition to ovals, variations of other basic shapes—such as circles, squares, rectangles, triangles, and simple lines—are used to connect the shapes. Using these basic shapes will help you start your drawing.

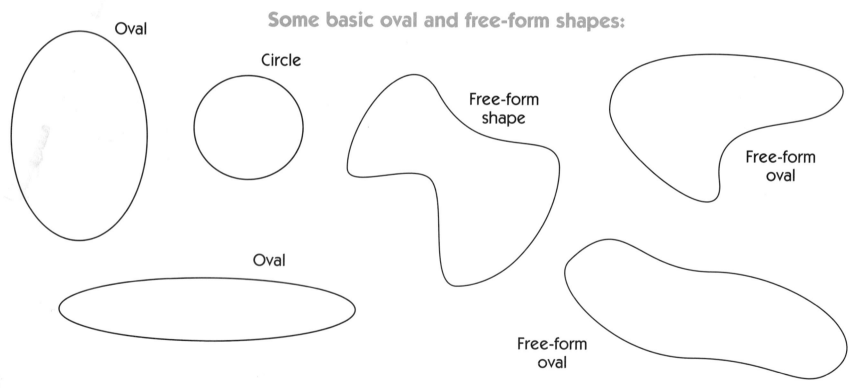

Some basic oval and free-form shapes:

Oval

Circle

Free-form shape

Free-form oval

Oval

Free-form oval

SUPPLIES

NUMBER-2 PENCILS
SOFT ERASER
DRAWING PAD

FELT-TIP PEN
COLORED PENCILS
MARKERS OR CRAYONS

HELPFUL HINTS

1. Take your time with steps 1 and 2. Following the first steps carefully will make the final steps easier. The first two steps create a solid foundation of the figure—much like a builder, who must construct a foundation before building the rest of the house. Next comes the fun part: creating the smooth, clean outline drawing of the animal and adding all the finishing touches, details, shading, and color.

2. Always keep your pencil lines light and soft. This will make your guidelines easier to erase when you no longer need them.

3. Don't be afraid to erase. It usually takes a lot of drawing and erasing before you will be satisfied with the way your drawing looks.

4. Add details, shading and all the finishing touches *after* you have blended and refined all the shapes and your figure is complete.

5. Remember: Practice makes perfect. Don't be discouraged if you don't get the hang of it right away. Just keep drawing, erasing, and redrawing until you do.

HOW TO START

Look at the finished drawing below, #4. Study it. Then study the steps that were taken to get to the final drawing. Notice where the shapes overlap and where they align. Is the eye over the corner of the mouth or behind it? Look for relationships among the shapes.

Step 1. Draw the main shape first—usually, it's the largest. In this case, it is a large, free-form oval for the body. Then draw an oval for the head and connect it to the body, forming the neck. Use other basic shapes to add arms and claws.

Step 2. Carve out the dinosaur's mouth. Sketch additional basic shapes for the legs and tail.

Step 3. Blend and refine the shapes into a smooth outline of the dinosaur's body. Add the sharp teeth. Keep erasing and drawing until you feel that it is just right.

Tip: Dotted lines indicate guidelines that you will erase when you no longer need them (in this case, in step 3).

Step 4. Add lots of lines for shading and skin texture. Or you may choose to color your drawing with colored pencils, markers, or crayons.

Sometimes, it is helpful to start by tracing the final drawing to get an overall sense of the drawing's shape and size. Once you understand the relationships of the shapes and parts within the final drawing, you will find it easier to draw from scratch.

Remember: It is *not* important to get it perfect. It *is* important for you to be happy with your work!

Erasing Tips

• Once you have completed the line drawing (usually, after step #2), erase your guidelines. Then add details, shading, and/or color to your drawing.

• Using a permanent, fine-line marker over pencil lines you want to keep will make it easier to erase guidelines.

• A very soft or kneaded eraser will erase the pencil lines without smudging the drawing or ripping the paper.

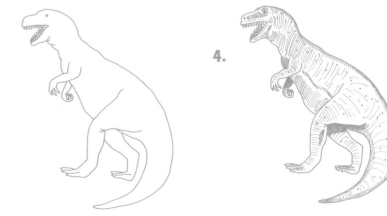

1.   2.   3.   4.

BASIC DINOSAUR CLASSIFICATION

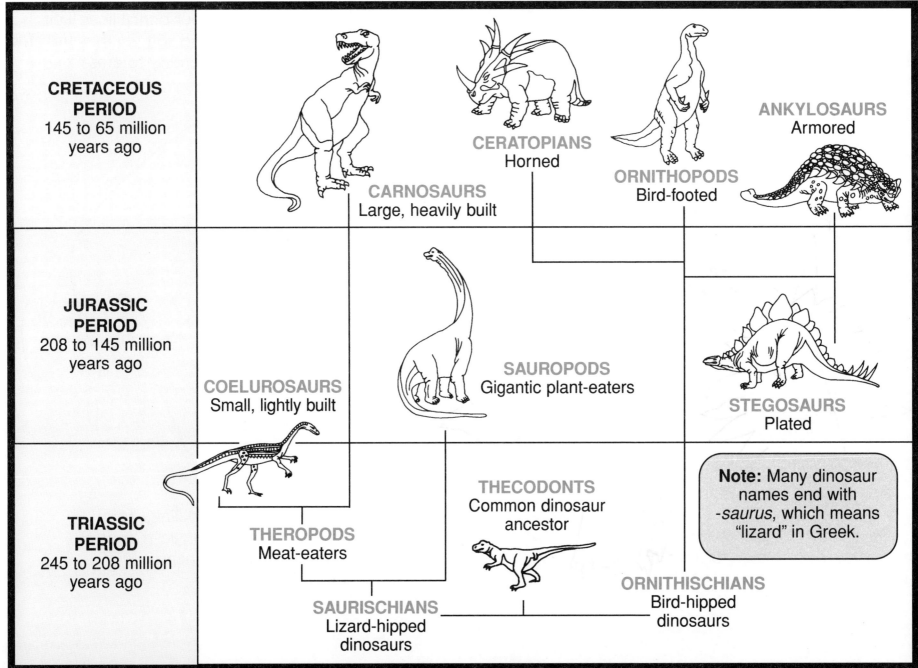

CRETACEOUS PERIOD
145 to 65 million years ago

JURASSIC PERIOD
208 to 145 million years ago

TRIASSIC PERIOD
245 to 208 million years ago

CARNOSAURS
Large, heavily built

CERATOPIANS
Horned

ORNITHOPODS
Bird-footed

ANKYLOSAURS
Armored

COELUROSAURS
Small, lightly built

SAUROPODS
Gigantic plant-eaters

STEGOSAURS
Plated

THECODONTS
Common dinosaur ancestor

Note: Many dinosaur names end with *-saurus*, which means "lizard" in Greek.

THEROPODS
Meat-eaters

SAURISCHIANS
Lizard-hipped dinosaurs

ORNITHISCHIANS
Bird-hipped dinosaurs

STYRACOSAURUS

(sty-RAK-uh-SORE-us)

Hint: Always keep your pencil lines light and soft, so they will be easy to erase.

The name means "spiked lizard," because of the spikes on this dinosaur's head. *Styracosaurus* was a plant-eater that may have lived in herds, grazing the fields like the American buffalo of the modern world.

1. Start with a large free-form oval for the body. Add shapes for the head, lower jaw, and pointed "beak."

2. Next, using simple guidelines, form the legs, tail, and the triangle-shaped spikes on the dinosaur's head.

3. Add an eye, then a small spike above it, as shown. Combine the shapes into a smooth outline of the body. Now you're ready for the finishing touches.

4. Complete the eye and beak. Then add lots of shading and skin details. You can even add some ground for *Styracosaurus* to stomp on! For a dramatic effect, try going over the outline with a felt-tip pen.

ORNITHOMIMUS
(OR-nith-uh-MY-mus)

The name means "bird imitator," because this dinosaur resembled an ostrich. *Ornithomimus* was very speedy and ran quickly from danger.

1. Start your drawing with a large free-form oval for the body and a smaller one for the head. Create the neck by sketching lines to join the two ovals.

2. Using simple basic shapes, draw the tail, arms, and legs as shown.

3. Form the mouth and eye. Then blend the guideline shapes into a smooth outline, erasing unneeded lines as you go along.

4. Add claws to the fingers and toes. Then sketch lots of shading lines and skin texture for the finishing touches.

Hint: Before going on to step 4, make sure that you are satisfied with the way your drawing looks. If you aren't, don't hesitate to erase and redraw it.

PALAEOSCINCUS

(PAY-lee-oh-SKINK-us)

The name means "ancient skink," because the teeth resemble those of a modern skink (a type of lizard). *Palaeoscincus* was discovered when scientists found one tooth in Montana.

1. Begin this dinosaur with a large oval shape for the body and two overlapping circles for the head. Attach the tail, adding two egg-shaped ovals at the tip.

2. Add the legs and claws. Next, carefully add rows of triangle-shaped spikes all over the body and tail. Don't forget the four spikes protecting the head.

Hint: Steps 1 and 2 are very important. They establish the overall structure and look of your drawing. In steps 3 and 4, you will simply refine and add details to the figure you create in steps 1 and 2.

10

3. Complete the face, then blend all the separate shapes into a smooth outline of the dinosaur's body. Be sure to erase any lines you no longer need.

4. Now use your imagination to fill in the details. What color or colors do you think this dinosaur was? No one really knows, so use your favorite colors to complete *Palaeoscincus*.

DIPLODOCUS
(dih-PLOH-duh-kus)

The name, which means "double beam," refers to the *Y*-shaped vertebrae on the tail. A complete skeleton of *Diplodocus* measured 90 feet from head to tail. Many of this plant-eater's bones have been found in the Rocky Mountain states of North America.

1. By drawing *Diplodocus* at the angle shown, you can get a better sense of how gigantic this dinosaur was. Start with a very large oval for the body. Add a small circle for the chest and a small oval with a circle on top for the head. Connect the head and body with two long, curving lines, forming the neck.

2. Draw the rectangular-shaped legs and attach the huge, curved tail.

3. Add the eye and mouth. Then blend all your shapes into one finished outline drawing. Erase any extra lines.

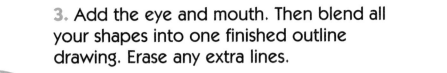

4. Add details, background, and color. You may want to create a scene by drawing several different dinosaurs in a prehistoric setting. (For help with scenery, see pages 90-91.)

Hint: Focus on one part of the body at a time. Keep sketching and erasing until you are satisfied before moving on to the next part.

VELOCIRAPTOR

(vuh-LAH-sih-RAP-tur)

The name means "swift robber," due to this dinosaur's quickness and its grasping hands. If *Velociraptor* was cold-blooded, its skin would have been similar to a lizard's. If it was warm-blooded, it may have been covered with feathers or fur.

1. Lightly sketch an egg-shaped oval for the body. Next, using oval guidelines, very carefully create the upper and lower jaws, then connect them to the body. Then add the tail.

2. Using simple shapes, draw the arms, legs, and claws. Note the upturned claw on each foot.

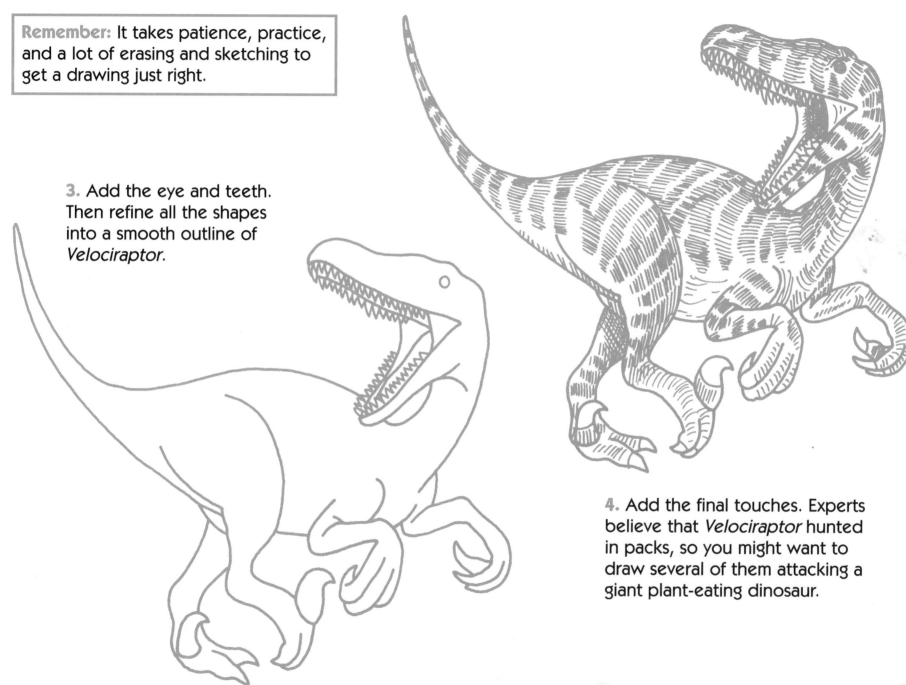

3. Add the eye and teeth. Then refine all the shapes into a smooth outline of *Velociraptor*.

4. Add the final touches. Experts believe that *Velociraptor* hunted in packs, so you might want to draw several of them attacking a giant plant-eating dinosaur.

COELOPHYSIS

(SEEL-uh-FYE-sis)

The name, which means "hollow form," refers to this dinosaur's hollow bones.

2. Blend your shapes into a body form. Add a long, slender tail. Then erase any lines you don't need.

1. Start your drawing with basic shapes for the head, neck, body, arms, and legs.

Hint: Add shading and other details only *after* you are satisfied with your body-form outline figure.

3. Finish your drawing by adding facial features, skin markings, and other details. Then color *Coelophysis* in bright colors.

ICHTHYOSAUR
(IK-thee-oh-sore)

The name means "fish lizard," referring to the fishlike appearance. This animal was a prehistoric sea reptile, not a dinosaur. Unlike dinosaurs, ichthyosaurs gave birth to live young.

1. Lightly sketch the basic shapes— an oval for the body, triangles for the head and fins, and a curving oval for the tail section. Add the eye.

Hint: Dotted lines show guidelines that will be erased.

2. Curve and blend the separate shapes into a smooth body outline. Erase any lines you no longer need.

3. Complete the eye. Then add some shading and skin patterns. Does the ichthyosaur remind you of any modern sea animal?

HADROSAURUS
(HAD-ruh-SORE-us)

The name means "bulky lizard," referring to the animal's big size. In 1868, a plaster skeleton of a *Hadrosaurus* was the first dinosaur ever put on display.

1. Draw a large oval for the body and a smaller, pointy-ended oval for the head. Connect the two ovals to form the neck. Then attach a long triangle for the tail.

Remember: It is easy to draw almost anything if you first break it down into simple shapes.

2. Add a line for the mouth. Next, using ovals, rectangles, and triangles, add guideline shapes for the arms and legs.

3. Add the eye, then blend the other shapes into a smooth body outline. Note the flattened snout. Keep erasing and drawing until you are satisfied with the way your dinosaur looks.

4. Create the pointy claws and complete the eye. Then add lots of shading, skin wrinkles, some color, and scenery to complete your picture.

CERATOSAURUS
(suh-RAT-oh-SORE-us)

The name, which means "horned lizard," refers to the horn behind the nose. Meat-eating *Ceratosaurus* was found at the scene of a crime in Wyoming: Its broken teeth were lying next to a fossilized *Camarasaurus* skeleton.

1. Begin by sketching a large, free-form oval for the body and a smaller oval for the head. Connect the ovals to form the neck.

2. Add the horn and open mouth to the head. Next, using basic guideline shapes, lightly draw the arms, hands, legs, and feet. Then add the curved tail.

3. Add the eye and sharp teeth. Then sketch and erase to blend all the shapes together, erasing any unneeded guidelines.

Hint: Feel free to use your imagination when adding final details and scenery.

4. Add details and shading for the finishing touches. You can outline *Ceratosaurus* with a black felt-tip pen or color it with your favorite colors.

IGUANODON
(ih-GWAHN-uh-don)

The name means "iguana tooth," because the teeth resemble those of an iguana lizard. About 140 million years ago, a large number of *Iguanodons* drowned in a lake that ran across northwest Europe. Many fossils have been found in this "Iguanodon graveyard."

2. Add the basic shapes for the arms, legs, pointy claws, and tail. Note the spike pointing upward on top of each hand. Don't forget the mouth!

1. Start with a large free-form oval for the body. Add a smaller oval for the head and a triangle shape for most of the neck. Connect the neck and body with a short line, as shown.

Hint: Make sure that you have built a solid foundation with the first two steps before going on to step 3.

3. Add an eye and a nostril. Then erase unneeded guidelines as you blend the shapes and lines into a smooth outline of *Iguanodon*.

4. Complete your drawing by adding rows of shading and skin details. Now this *Iguanodon* is ready to pound the prehistoric pavement!

AVIMIMUS
(ah-vee-MEEM-us)

The name means "bird mimic," due to this dinosaur's birdlike appearance. Some experts believe that *Avimimus* was similar to the modern-day roadrunner, and that it might have had feathers.

Hint: This dinosaur may seem difficult to draw, but if you work carefully, one step at a time, you will be able to draw almost anything.

1. Lightly sketch a free-form shape for the body. Add the head, neck, and tail as shown.

2. Draw some simple shapes to create the arms, claws, legs, and feet. Shape the head and define the open mouth.

24

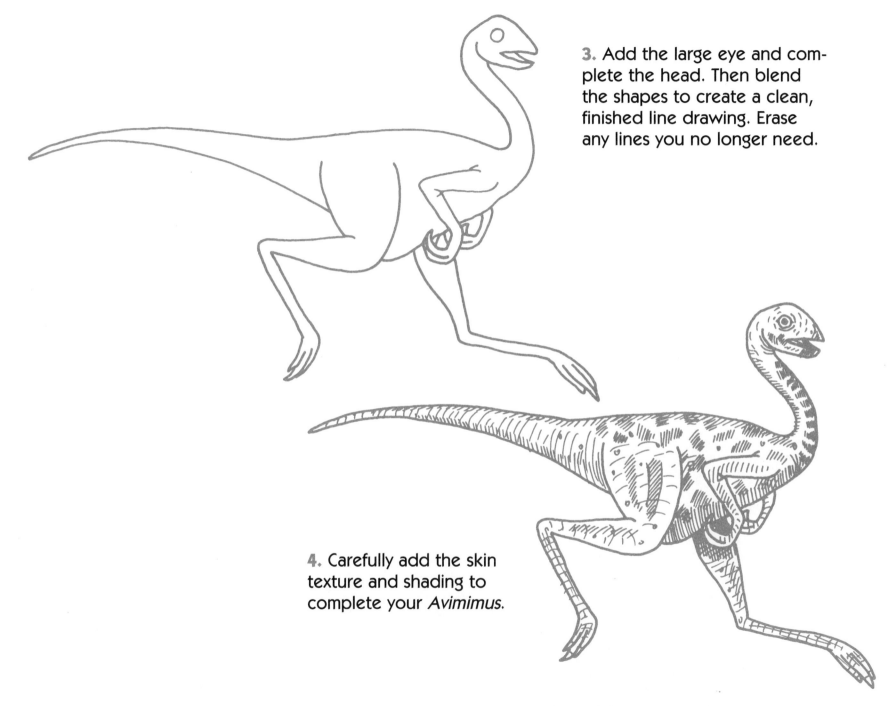

3. Add the large eye and complete the head. Then blend the shapes to create a clean, finished line drawing. Erase any lines you no longer need.

4. Carefully add the skin texture and shading to complete your *Avimimus*.

OVIRAPTOR
(OH-vee-RAP-tur)

The name means "egg stealer," because the fossilized bones were found near another dinosaur's nest of eggs. The shape of *Oviraptor*'s head tells us that it probably used its deep beak and two sharp teeth to break eggshells. Its eyes are set far apart, which would have helped this dinosaur watch for danger while it ate.

1. Use a free-form oval as the basic guideline shape for the body. Draw a smaller one for the head then connect it to the body, forming the neck. Add shapes for the bent arm.

Remember: Keep all your lines and shapes lightly drawn.

2. Using additional basic shapes, create the legs and tail. (Note the downward-shaped spikes behind the feet.) Draw the open mouth.

3. Add an eye, a nostril, and a tiny hole at the jaw. Connect and blend all the lines into a smooth body shape, erasing unnecessary lines as you go along.

4. Shading and skin texture will give your *Oviraptor* a dramatic effect.

TYLOSAURUS

(TY-loh-SORE-us)

Tylosaurus—not a dinosaur—was one of the largest known seagoing lizards. Close in appearance to a modern crocodile, it was a hunter of fish and shellfish.

2. Add the long, curving tail. Then use basic oval shapes to create the row of back scales.

1. Carefully draw the basic body shape. Add a small circle for the head and two triangles for the huge mouth. Next, add four ovals for the flippers, attaching them to the body with connector lines.

4. Once you are satisfied with your step 3 drawing, add the finishing touches—including lines to create shading and texture—to complete your *Tylosaurus*.

3. Add the teeth. Then sketch and erase to blend all the shapes into a continuous body outline.

Remember: Practice makes perfect. Keep drawing and erasing until you are satisfied with the way your picture looks.

LAMBEOSAURUS

(LAM-bee-uh-SORE-us)

The name means "Lambe's Lizard," in honor of Lawrence Lambe, who studied dinosaur fossils. *Lambeosaurus* was a crested duckbill dinosaur. The hollow crest on its head may have been used to make loud noises.

2. Carefully add the crest on top of the head with a rectangle and a small oval. Then, using basic guideline shapes, lightly sketch the arms, hands, legs, feet, and tail.

1. Start by sketching a large oval for the body, then a circle and triangle for the head. Connect the two ovals.

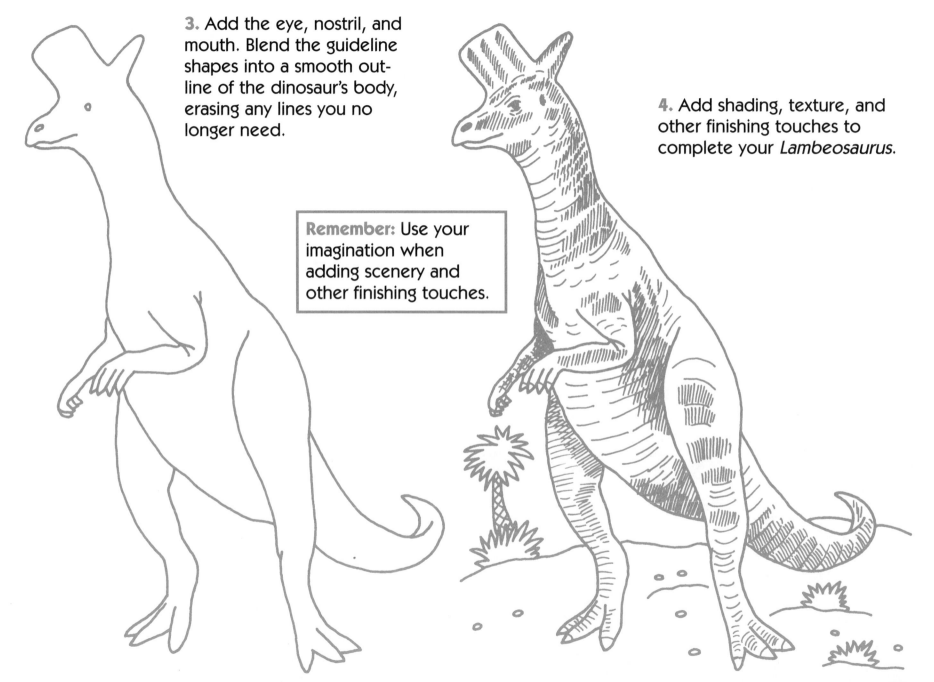

3. Add the eye, nostril, and mouth. Blend the guideline shapes into a smooth outline of the dinosaur's body, erasing any lines you no longer need.

4. Add shading, texture, and other finishing touches to complete your *Lambeosaurus*.

Remember: Use your imagination when adding scenery and other finishing touches.

ALLOSAURUS

(AL-uh-SORE-us)

The name means "different lizard," because the bones of the spine were different from other dinosaurs'. *Allosaurus* was a big, 40-foot-long, meat-eating dinosaur. It was quite active for its size.

1. Start your drawing with a large, bean-shaped oval for the body. Lightly sketch a smaller oval for the head, then connect them to form the neck. Then add a small oval guideline where the eye will go.

2. Draw the open mouth. Then, using basic shapes, carefully attach the arms, legs, and tail.

3. Add the teeth and eye. Then blend the lines and shapes into a smooth, clean outline. As you work, erase any guidelines you no longer need.

Remember: Keep sketching and erasing until you are satisfied with the way your drawing looks—especially in step 3.

4. Finish *Allosaurus* by adding lots of detail. Shading, lines for wrinkles, and tiny shapes for the bumpy skin texture will give your drawing a realistic look. Don't forget some background scenery.

CHASMOSAURUS

(KAZ-moh-SORE-us)

The name means "opening lizard," describing the openings in this dinosaur's head frill. The large holes lightened the bony frill's weight. A plant-eater, *Chasmosaurus* was one of the most widespread dinosaurs. The bones of have been found in Texas and in Alberta, Canada.

1. Sketch a large bean-shaped oval for the body. Lightly sketch a smaller overlapping oval for the head. Then add a basic guideline shape for the tail.

2. Carefully draw the head frill as shown. Next, using basic shapes, attach the arms and legs.

34

3. Add an eye, then create the open mouth and nostril. Next, add two overlapping horns on the frill, and a smaller horn on the front of the head. Blend the shapes into a smooth, clean outline. Erase any unneeded guidelines.

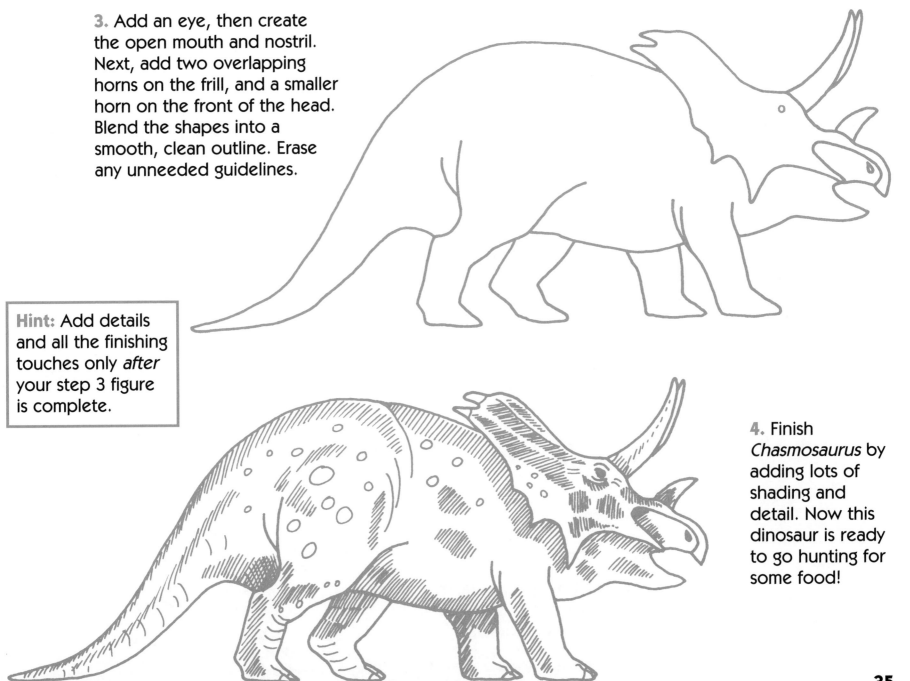

Hint: Add details and all the finishing touches only *after* your step 3 figure is complete.

4. Finish *Chasmosaurus* by adding lots of shading and detail. Now this dinosaur is ready to go hunting for some food!

TROODON
(TROH-oh-don)

The name, which means "wounding tooth," refers to this dinosaur's sharp, serrated, sharklike teeth.

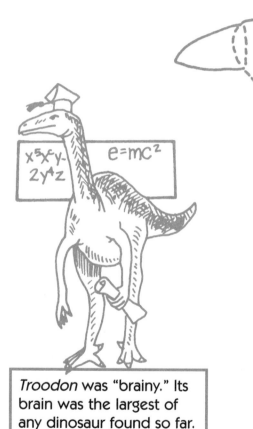

Troodon was "brainy." Its brain was the largest of any dinosaur found so far.

Hint: Before you begin, study the finished drawing in step 4, so you will be familiar with this dinosaur as you sketch the basic shapes.

1. Using basic guideline shapes, lightly draw the body, neck, head, beak, and tail.

2. Attach basic shapes for the arms, hands, legs, and feet. Then create the beak.

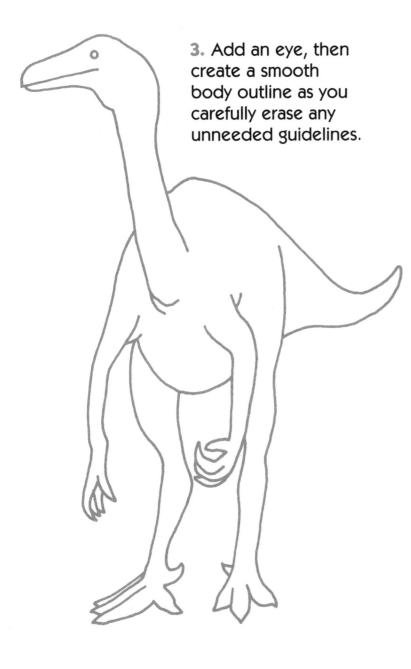

3. Add an eye, then create a smooth body outline as you carefully erase any unneeded guidelines.

4. Add details, such as short claws to the fingers and toes. After you add skin texture and shading, your *Troodon* will be ready to join other dinosaurs you've drawn in a prehistoric scene!

ARCHAEOPTERYX

(AR-kee-OP-ter-iks)

The name means "ancient wing," because many experts believe that this animal was one of the first birds. *Archaeopteryx* fossils formed in limestone in Germany show impressions of long feathers on the wings and tail.

Hint: This drawing may appear more difficult than most, but if you follow along carefully, step by step, you will soon be satisfied with your work.

1. Draw an oval for the body, then a small circle for the head. Connect them to form the neck. Then add two overlapping triangles for the beak.

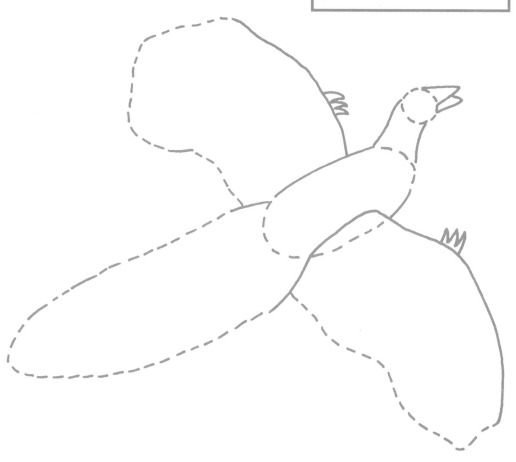

2. Add three large guideline shapes for the wings and tail feathers. Then add claws, which stick out at the front of each wing.

3. Carefully form curved feathers around the edges of the wings and tail. Next, draw dotted lines on each wing as shown. Add the eye and nostril. Then blend the shapes into one smooth body outline, erasing any lines you no longer need.

4. Using the dotted lines as your guide, add two more rows of feathers to each wing. This part is fun to do! Make the outer wing and tail feathers longer. Then add shading and details to complete your drawing.

OURANOSAURUS
(oo-RAN-oh-SORE-us)

The name means "valiant lizard," after a West African word for "fearless." A relative of *Iguanodon*, *Ouranosaurus* had a sail on its back, probably to keep it from overheating.

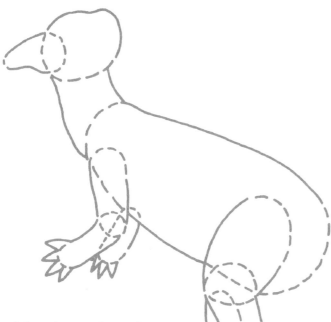

1. Start with a large free-form oval for the body. Add the head and pointed "beak," then connect them to the body. Next, use simple shapes to draw the arms and legs.

2. Attach a long curvy tail. Then create the sail by sketching a line from behind the head to halfway down the tail. Add oval shapes to the sail as shown.

Hint: Steps 1 and 2 establish the overall structure and look of your drawing. In steps 3 and 4, you will simply refine and add details.

3. Add an eye, then work on blending the guideline shapes together. Erase unneeded lines as you go along.

4. When you're satisfied with the way your *Ouranosaurus* looks, add lines for shading, or color the dinosaur with your choice of colors.

BRACHIOSAURUS
(BRAK-ee-uh-SORE-us)

The name means "arm lizard," referring to the long front legs. The tiny head of *Brachiosaurus* had huge nostrils on top. They may have helped to keep the dinosaur cool.

1. Lightly sketch the basic guideline shapes—ovals, rectangles, and triangles—for the body, legs, and feet.

2. High above the body, draw the head, using a small oval and a circle. Connect the head to the body with two long, curved lines. Then use more simple, basic shapes to add the tail.

3. Add the mouth and eye. Blend the shapes into a continuous smooth outline, erasing unnecessary guidelines as you go along.

Remember: Focus on one part of the body at a time, sketching and erasing until you are satisfied with that part.

4. Lots of interesting shading will make your *Brachiosaurus* come alive. What color do you think this dinosaur was?

PSITTACOSAURUS

(SIT-ak-oh-SORE-us)

The name means "parrot lizard," for this dinosaur's parrot-shaped head. Scientists think that little *Psittacosaurus* belonged to a group of dinosaurs that were the ancestors of Ceratopians—large, big-horned dinosaurs, such as *Triceratops*.

1. Use a free-form oval as the basic guideline shape for the body. Attach the tail. Next, draw a small oval with an overlapping circle for the head. Then connect it to the body, forming the neck. Sketch in the open mouth.

2. Add simple shapes to form the arms, claws, and legs.

Remember: Keep all your lines lightly drawn, so they will be easy to erase later.

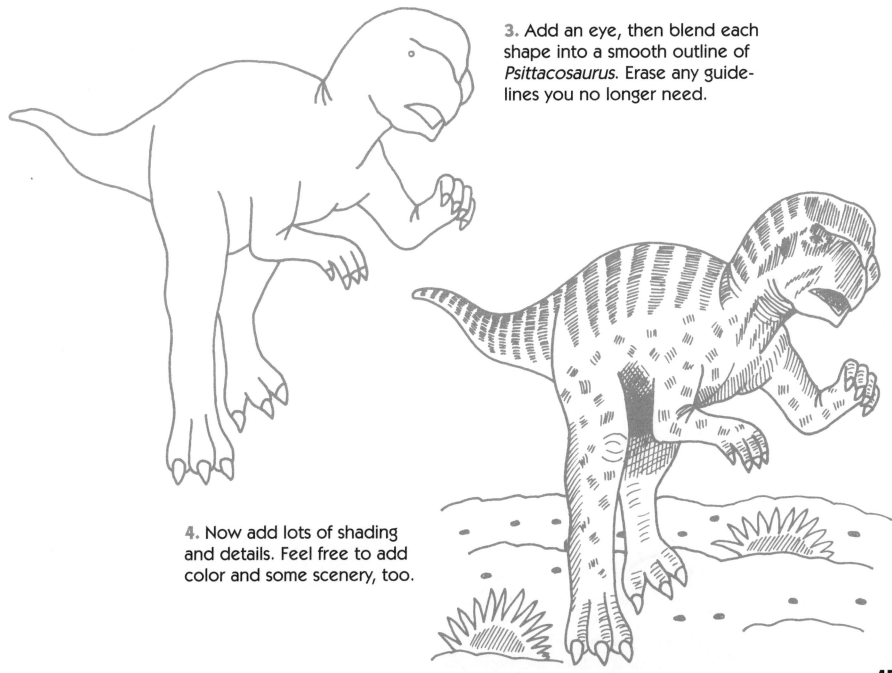

3. Add an eye, then blend each shape into a smooth outline of *Psittacosaurus*. Erase any guidelines you no longer need.

4. Now add lots of shading and details. Feel free to add color and some scenery, too.

MEGALOSAURUS

(MEG-ah-loh-SORE-us)

The name, which means "big lizard," refers to this animal's size. *Megalosaurus* was the first dinosaur to be described and named, early in the 19th century.

Remember: Dotted lines show guidelines that can be erased when they are no longer needed.

1. Begin by drawing the basic shapes for the body and head. Sketch lines to connect the head and body, forming the neck. Add more basic shapes for the arms and hands.

2. Add the basic shapes for the legs and tail. Then sketch and erase to create the open mouth, as shown.

3. Add the eye and sharp teeth. Next, blend all the shapes together, erasing any lines you no longer need. Don't go to step 4 until you are satisfied with the way the outline drawing looks.

4. Add details and shading to complete this fierce-looking, meat-eating dinosaur.

ANATOSAURUS
(ah-NAT-uh-SORE-us)

The name means "duck lizard," referring to this dinosaur's flat, ducklike bill. Fossil impressions of *Anatosaurus* show that it had rough, pebbly skin.

1. Begin by lightly sketching two oval guideline shapes for the body. Then add the head, duckbill, neck, and tail.

2. Add the eye and simple shapes for the arm and legs.

3. Sketch and erase to blend all the guidelines into one clean, basic body shape, erasing extra lines as you go along.

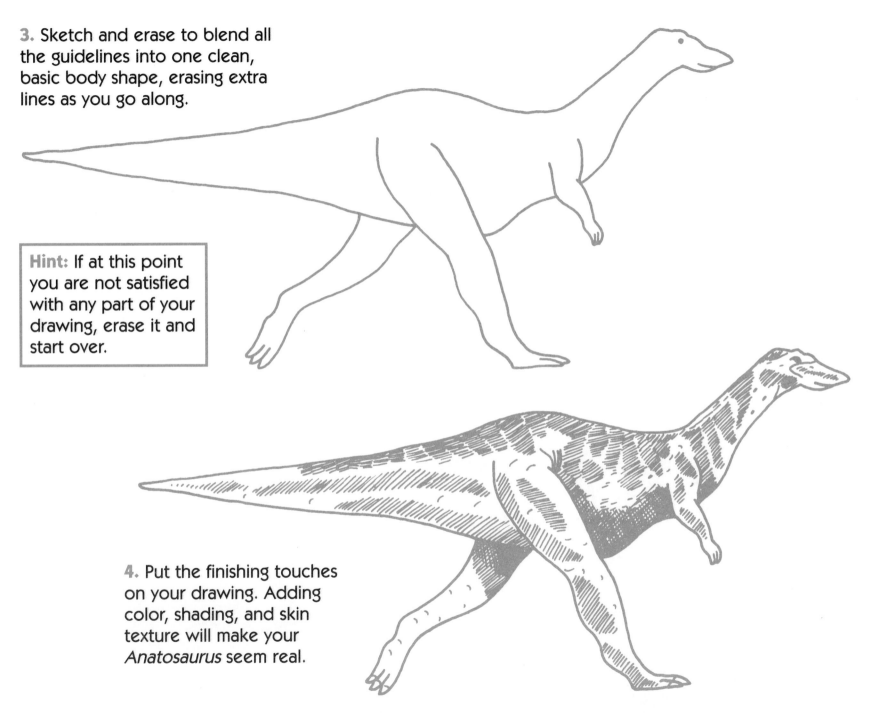

Hint: If at this point you are not satisfied with any part of your drawing, erase it and start over.

4. Put the finishing touches on your drawing. Adding color, shading, and skin texture will make your *Anatosaurus* seem real.

LEPTOCERATOPS

(LEP-toe-SER-uh-tops)

The name means "slender-horned face," for this dinosaur's appearance.

1. Lightly sketch the basic guideline shapes—oval for the body and triangles for the head and tail. Connect the head to the body. Add a small triangle for the beak and a short line for the mouth.

2. Attach the shapes for the arms and legs.

3. Starting with the head, combine, blend, and define the shapes into a clean outline drawing. Erase unneeded guidelines.

Hint: Practice makes perfect. Don't be discouraged if you don't get the hang of it right away. Just keep erasing and sketching until you do.

4. Complete this dinosaur's features and add shading and skin texture. Use your imagination to color your drawing.

Leptoceratops was a member of the horned dinosaur family. However, it had no horns and had only a small frill around its neck.

DILOPHOSAURUS

(dye-LOH-fuh-SORE-us)

The name means "two-crested lizard" because of the two crests on this dinosaur's head. Unlike other big meat-eaters, *Dilophosaurus* had bone joints that would have allowed it to wrinkle its nose.

Remember: It usually is easier to draw the largest shape first.

1. Start by drawing two free-form ovals—one for the body and one for the head. Connect the ovals, then add the tail.

2. Next, add basic shapes for the arms, claws, legs, and feet. Draw the open mouth, then add the two crests on the head.

3. Add an eye and a nostril. Blend the lines and shapes into a smooth outline of *Dilophosaurus*. Then add lots of pointy teeth.

4. Now add all the final touches. Spots, shading, and skin wrinkles will make this dinosaur look ferociously real.

HYLAEOSAURUS

(HY-lee-oh-SORE-us)

The name means "wood lizard," because of the place in England where it was found. Armored *Hylaeosaurus* lived near a body of water that formed as the continents drifted apart during the early Cretaceous period.

2. Add an oval for the mouth and a circle for the snout. Then, sketching carefully, add the rows of triangular spikes on the dinosaur's back and tail.

1. Draw a large free-form oval as the basic guideline shape for the body. Draw a smaller overlapping oval for the head. Add more simple shapes for the legs, feet, and tail.

3. Add the eye, then complete the mouth and snout. Blend the shapes together, erasing unneeded lines as you go along.

Hint: Breaking down complicated areas into simple shapes makes them easier to draw.

4. Add teeth, plus lots of other details, wrinkles, and color to complete your *Hylaeosaurus*.

55

DEINONYCHUS
(dye-NON-ih-kus)

The name means "terrible claw" because of the giant, curved claw on top of each foot. Wolf-sized *Deinonychus*, a meat-eater, may have hunted in packs.

Remember: Keep all your lines lightly drawn. It will be easier to erase them later.

1. Draw a large oval for the body, then a smaller oval for the head. Connect the two ovals to form the neck. Attach a long triangle for the tail.

2. Create the mouth. Then, using simple guideline shapes, sketch the arms, legs, and claws. Note the large, curved claw on top of each foot.

3. Add the eye, nostril, and sharp teeth. Starting with the head, blend the shapes into an outline drawing of this fierce, meat-eating dinosaur. Keep drawing, erasing, and redrawing until you are satisfied with this stage of your drawing.

4. Now add the finishing touches. Careful use of shading, skin texture, and color will make *Deinonychus* come alive!

ANTARCTOSAURUS
(ant-ARK-toh-SORE-us)

The name means "southern lizard," because this dinosaur's remains were found on the southern tip of South America. Fossils of *Antarctosaurus* were also found in India, raising a question as to when the continents separated.

1. Start with a large free-form oval for the body, then sketch a smaller one for the head. Add a small circle where the eye will go, and a short line for the mouth. Create the long, curved neck by joining the two ovals. Then add the tail.

2. Draw the basic shapes for the legs and feet.

3. Add the nostril. Then blend the basic body shapes together as you erase guidelines you no longer need.

4. Finish your drawing by adding details, such as skin textures, shading, and color.

ALBERTOSAURUS
(al-BUR-tuh-SORE-us)

The name means "Alberta lizard," after the area in Canada where it was found. A relative of *Tyrannosaurus*, *Albertosaurus* is also known as *Gorgosaurus*.

1. Begin by sketching a simple oval body. Add the head, neck, and tail as shown.

Remember: Take your time doing steps 1 and 2. If you get them right, the rest of your drawing will be easy to do.

2. Using basic guideline shapes, draw the arms and legs. Then add the open mouth.

3. Blend and refine the guidelines into the basic body outline of *Albertosaurus*. Erase any lines you no longer need. Then give this ferocious dinosaur some sharp teeth.

4. Now put the final touches on your masterpiece. Don't forget the pointy claws and wrinkly skin! Add shading and—for more drama—some background scenery.

APATOSAURUS
(uh-PAT-uh-SORE-us)

The name means "deceptive lizard." At one time, this dinosaur was known as *Brontosaurus*.

1. Start *Apatosaurus* with a large, oval body and legs. Add a long neck with a small, oval head, then a long tail.

Hint: Studying the final-step drawing before you start will help you under-stand how the basic shapes relate to each other.

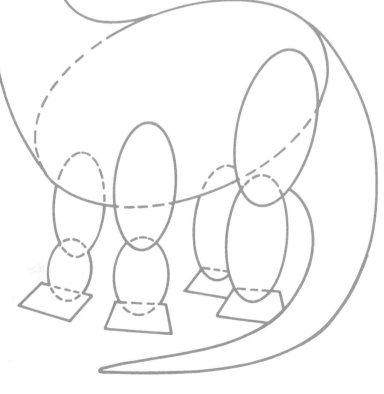

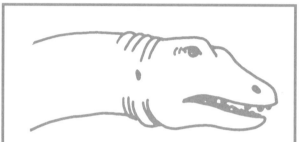

Apatosaurus was a plant-eater. It had small, peglike teeth that it used to strip leaves from tall trees.

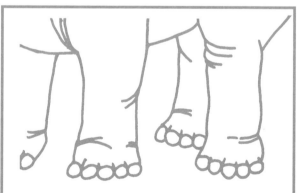

Apatosaurus had thick feet and legs. Its footprints measure nearly 36 inches long and 26 inches wide.

2. Blend all your shapes into one body shape. Erase any unnecessary lines.

3. Add lots of detail, shading, and texture. Put wrinkles on the skin surface, too! Draw some background scenery to complete your drawing.

PROTOCERATOPS

(PROH-toh-SER-uh-tops)

The name means "first horned face," because this was one of the first horned dinosaurs. *Protoceratops* was in the same family as *Triceratops*.

1. Start your drawing with three basic shapes for the head, body, and tail. Draw guideline shapes lightly.

2. Next, add four legs using ovals and triangles. Did you notice that the places where these shapes overlap and join are where body parts bend and move?

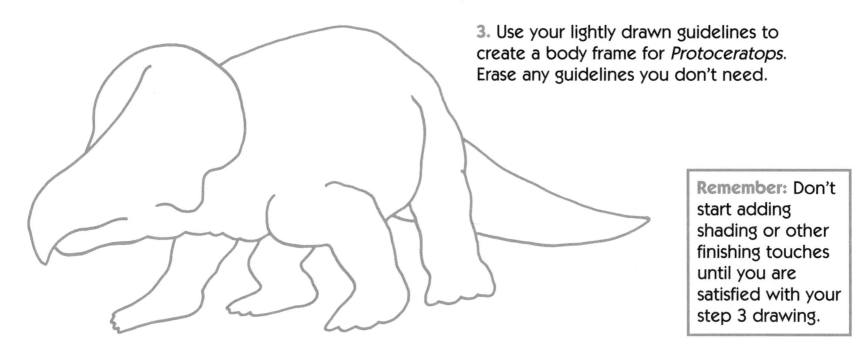

3. Use your lightly drawn guidelines to create a body frame for *Protoceratops*. Erase any guidelines you don't need.

Remember: Don't start adding shading or other finishing touches until you are satisfied with your step 3 drawing.

4. Add finishing touches to your drawing. Skin folds, textures, and shadings always make your dinosaur look more realistic. After you have learned to draw a few different dinosaurs, put them together in a scene. Stage a fight or see how many different dinosaurs you can fit on a page.

MAIASAURA
(MY-uh-SORE-uh)

The name means "good mother lizard," because this dinosaur's fossils were the first to suggest to experts that the females stayed with and cared for their offspring.

1. Lightly sketch a large oval for the body. Then add a small oval head and long neck.

Remember: Start by drawing the largest shape first.

2. Next, add a tail and four legs. Three legs are fully drawn, but the fourth leg is partially hidden behind another.

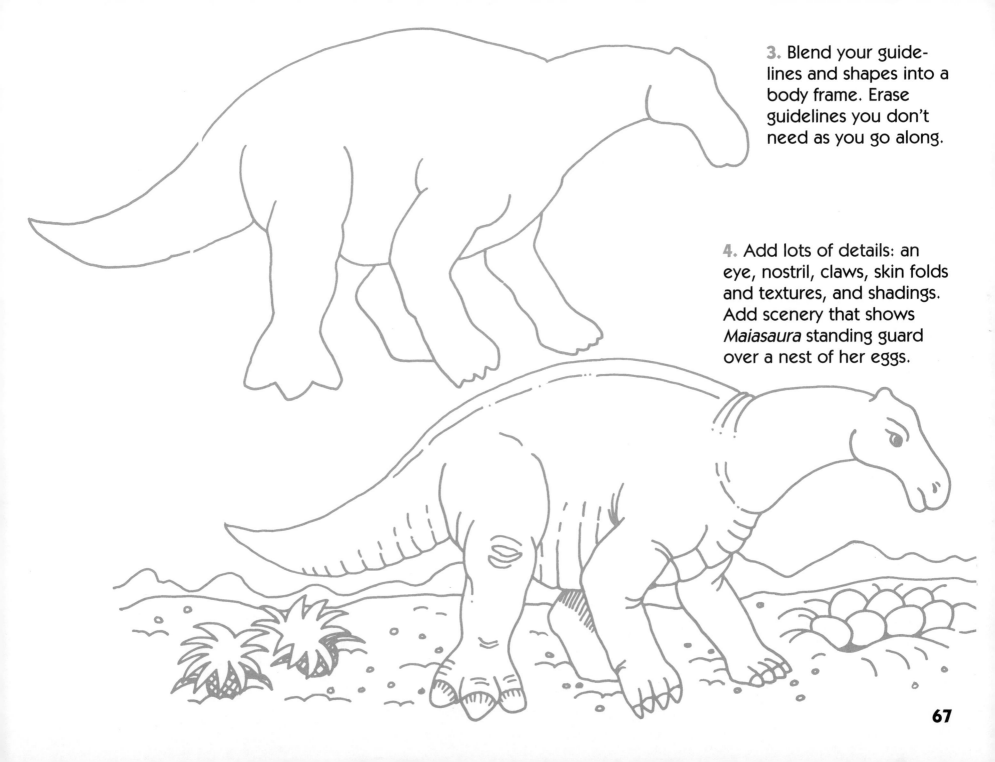

3. Blend your guide-lines and shapes into a body frame. Erase guidelines you don't need as you go along.

4. Add lots of details: an eye, nostril, claws, skin folds and textures, and shadings. Add scenery that shows *Maiasaura* standing guard over a nest of her eggs.

CORYTHOSAURUS
(koh-RITH-oh-SORE-us)

The name, which means "helmet lizard," refers to the shape of the bony crest on this dinosaur's head.

1. Start your dinosaur by sketching basic shapes (ovals and circles) for the head, neck, and body. These are only guidelines, so draw them lightly.

2. Next, add guidelines for the tail, legs, arms, and mouth. *Corythosaurus* had a mouth that looked like a duck's beak, and large, powerful legs to support its body.

Remember: Steps 1 and 2 are very important. It is easy to draw almost anything if you build a good foundation.

3. Blend the basic shapes into a clean outline, erasing guide-lines that you no longer need.

4. For the final step, add all the details. Draw in skin patterns, an eye, some claws, and skin folds. Then use your imagination to add some color.

The purpose of the bony crest on the head of *Corythosaurus* is unknown.

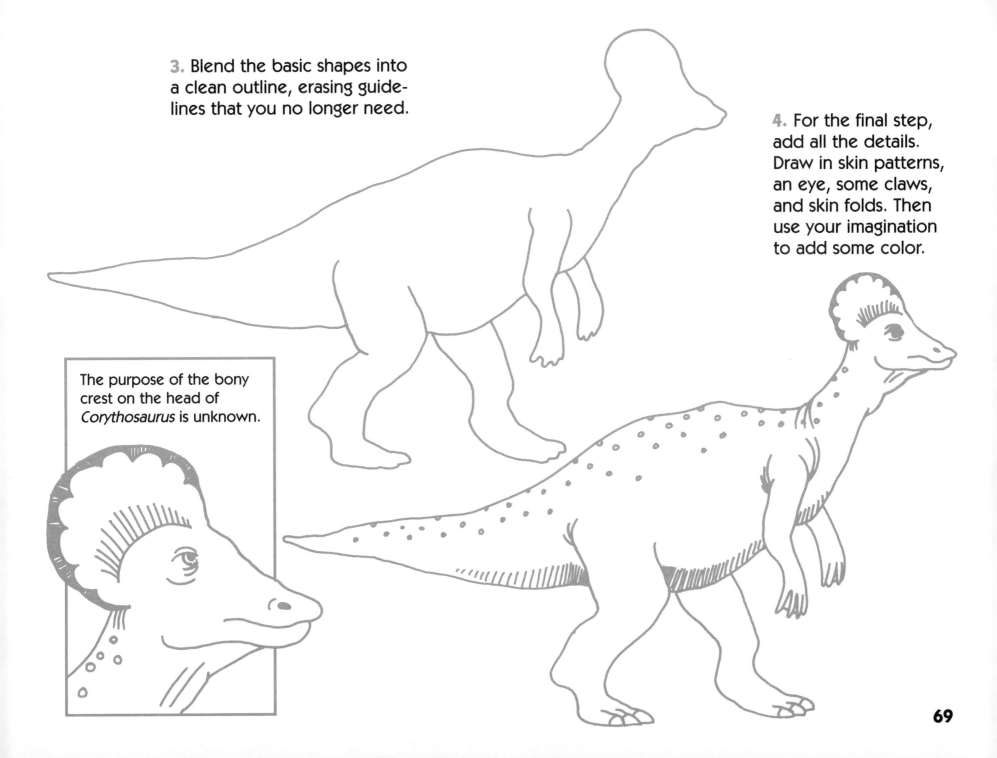

TYRANNOSAURUS
(ty-RAN-uh-SORE-us)

The name, which means "tyrant lizard," refers to its huge size and sharp teeth—signs that it was a fierce and mighty predator. It was one of the largest meat-eating dinosaurs. Only *Giganotosaurus (JIG-uh-NOT-oh-SORE-us)* and *Carcharodontosaurus (kar-KAR-oh-DON-tuh-SORE-us)* were larger.

2. Using basic shapes as your guide, add small forearms and large legs, as shown.

1. Use rectangles, ovals, squares, and triangles for the basic body, head, and tail. These are only guidelines, so draw them lightly.

3. Use your guidelines to form a clean outline of the basic body shape. As you work, erase any lines you don't need.

Hint: Once you learn to draw different dinosaurs, try making a whole dinosaur scene.

4. Put all the finishing touches on your drawing. Give *Tyrannosaurus* a ferocious look, big teeth, a mean look in its eye, and lots of skin effects. What color do you think *Tyrannosaurus* was? No one really knows, so let your imagination run wild!

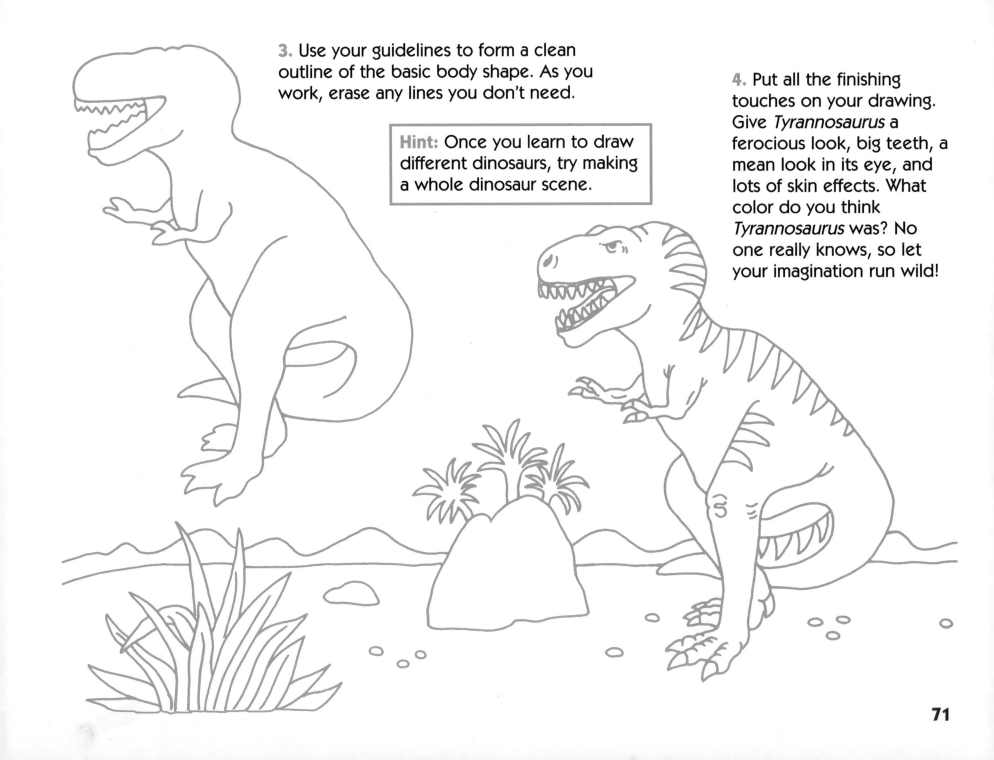

DROMAEOSAURUS
(DROH-mee-uh-SORE-us)

The name means "swift lizard," because this fast, fierce dinosaur ran upright on powerful legs.

1. Try to draw this dinosaur in just three steps. Use simple shapes for the body of your *Dromaeosaurus*. Lightly sketch the tail, neck, head, arms, and legs. Put some triangles in as guidelines for claws.

Dromaeosaurus had a large, razor-sharp, three-inch claw on each foot, used to slash and tear apart prey. When running, *Dromaeosaurus* held its claws upright.

Hint: Always draw your guidelines lightly—they'll be easier to erase.

2. Blend your basic shapes into a body shape while erasing guidelines you don't need.

3. Add an eye, a nostril, teeth, and claws. Then finish your *Dromaeosaurus* by adding important details, such as skin folds where the arms and legs bend. Use your imagination to draw in skin markings, textures, and colors.

STEGOSAURUS
(STEG-uh-SORE-us)

The name, which means "plated lizard," refers to the rows of plates on this dinosaur's back.

Hint: Each back plate is a basic diamond shape, with some hidden behind others. A diamond shape is made by putting two triangles together like this:

1. Start drawing your *Stegosaurus* by lightly sketching these basic shapes: first, a large oval, then two smaller ovals and a triangle.

2. Draw some triangles on the tail and diamond-shaped plates on the back. Add ovals for the legs and feet.

3. This step might look hard, but it's really easy. Take all your guidelines and blend them into this dinosaur's basic shape. Erase any unnecessary lines so that you have a clean line drawing of your *Stegosaurus*.

Make the tail horns curve.

4. Put the finishing touches on your drawing. Add texture to the back plates and some spots to *Stegosaurus*'s back.

SALTOPUS
(SAWL-toh-pus)

The name means "leaping foot," referring to the way *Saltopus* ran upright on its long hind legs. It was small—about the size of a house cat—and had five-fingered hands that made holding prey easier.

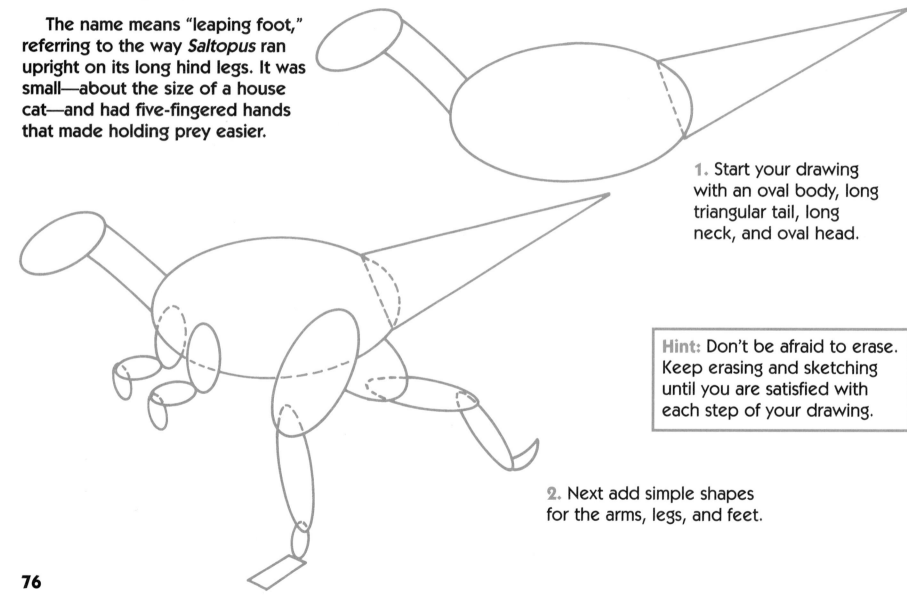

1. Start your drawing with an oval body, long triangular tail, long neck, and oval head.

Hint: Don't be afraid to erase. Keep erasing and sketching until you are satisfied with each step of your drawing.

2. Next add simple shapes for the arms, legs, and feet.

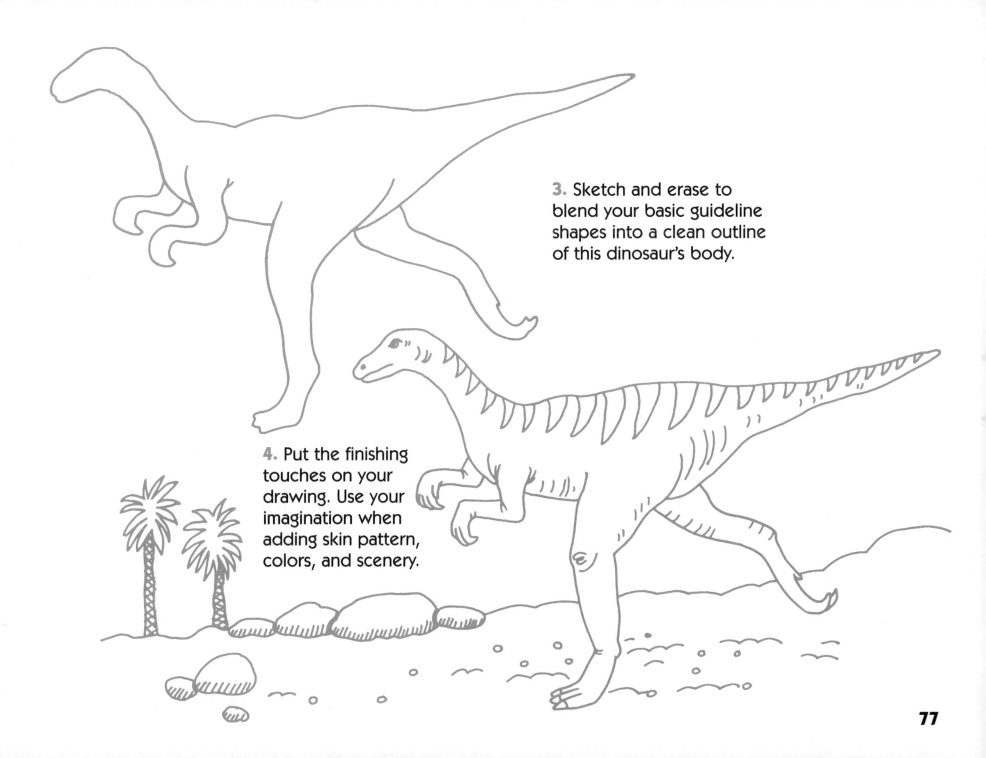

3. Sketch and erase to blend your basic guideline shapes into a clean outline of this dinosaur's body.

4. Put the finishing touches on your drawing. Use your imagination when adding skin pattern, colors, and scenery.

77

PARASAUROLOPHUS

(pah-ruh-saw-RAHL-uh-fus)

The name means "similar-crested lizard." No one knows the purpose of the bony crest on this dinosaur's head. Some experts think that it helped the animal's sense of smell. Others think that it was used to make loud noises.

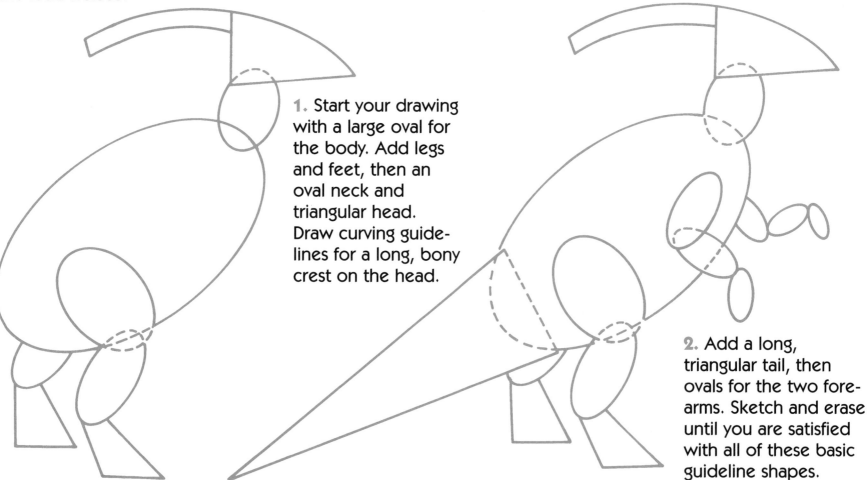

1. Start your drawing with a large oval for the body. Add legs and feet, then an oval neck and triangular head. Draw curving guidelines for a long, bony crest on the head.

2. Add a long, triangular tail, then ovals for the two forearms. Sketch and erase until you are satisfied with all of these basic guideline shapes.

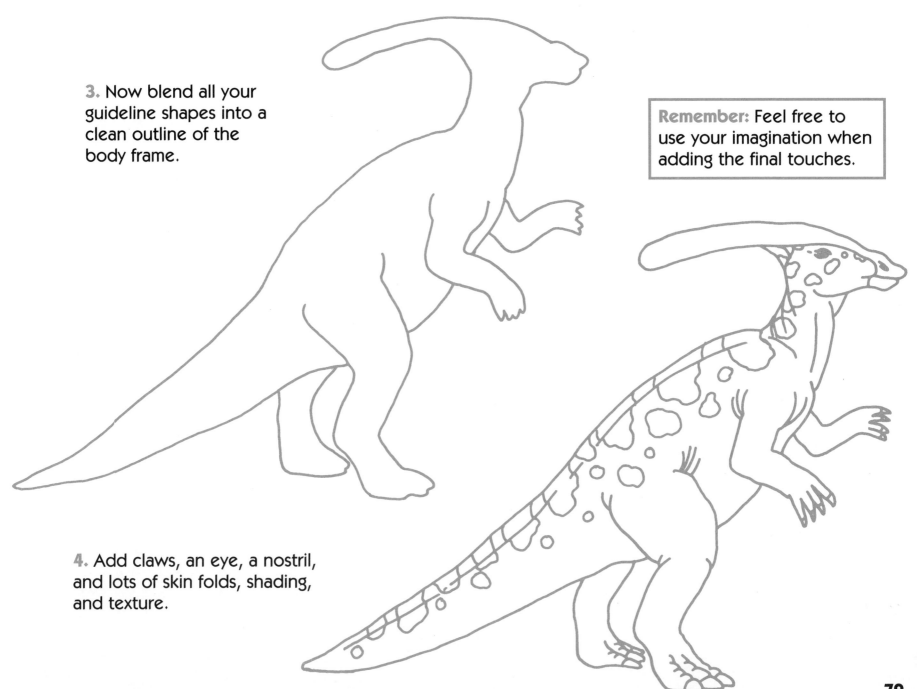

3. Now blend all your guideline shapes into a clean outline of the body frame.

4. Add claws, an eye, a nostril, and lots of skin folds, shading, and texture.

ANKYLOSAURUS
(ANG-kye-luh-SORE-us)

The name, which means "stiffened lizard," refers to this animal's hard, armor-plated body surface.

1. Start your *Ankylosaurus* with a large oval body. Use smaller ovals as guidelines for the head and legs. Then add triangles for the feet.

2. Next, add a long triangle for the tail, with an oval on the end. Don't forget to add some triangles all over its back, for the spikes.

3. Add more bumps to the the back as you refine the outline shape and erase guidelines.

Hint: In step 3, some lines get more curved, others get sharper.

4. Finish your drawing by adding claws, an eye, skin texture, and other details.

PTERANODON

(terr-AN-oh-dahn)

The name means "winged and toothless," because this animal could fly and had no teeth. *Pteranodon* was not a dinosaur—it was a Late Cretaceous flying reptile with a 25-foot wingspan.

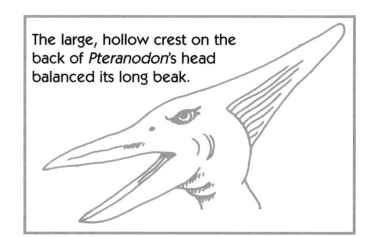

The large, hollow crest on the back of *Pteranodon*'s head balanced its long beak.

1. Start your drawing with simple shapes, as shown. Be sure to draw the wings much longer than the body.

Remember: Keep all your guidelines lightly drawn.

2. Next, draw guideline shapes for the arms, claws, and legs.

3. Sketch and erase to refine your drawing, then add the finishing details.

PACHYCEPHALOSAURUS

(pak-ee-SEFF-uh-loh-SORE-us)

The name, which means "reptile with a thick head," refers to the 10-inch-thick bone on top of this animal's head. Experts think that this dinosaur used its thick skull in head-butting contests.

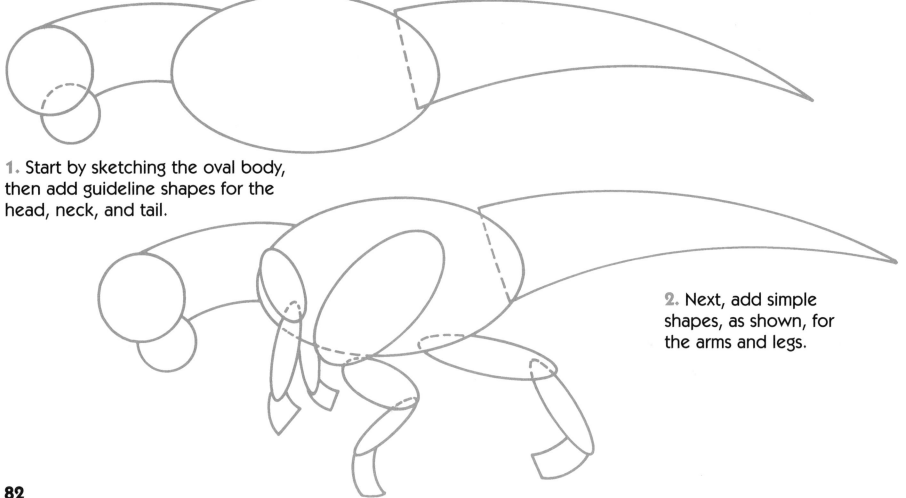

1. Start by sketching the oval body, then add guideline shapes for the head, neck, and tail.

2. Next, add simple shapes, as shown, for the arms and legs.

3. Sketch and erase to blend the separate guideline shapes into a clean outline of the body frame. Keep the head, neck, back, and tail in a straight line—this dinosaur is posed in head-butting position. As you work, erase unneeded guidelines.

Remember: If you are not satisfied with any part of your step 3 drawing, erase it and start over.

4. Now add the finishing touches: some spots on the skin; bony, bumpy texture on the head and nose; and lots of skin wrinkles. Why not add some scenery—and a second *Pachycephalosaurus* facing this one, ready for battle?

TRICERATOPS

(try-SER-uh-tops)

The name means "three-horned face." This animal was one of the last dinosaurs to become extinct.

1. Start drawing *Triceratops* by sketching a large circle for the body. Then add an oval and triangles, as shown.

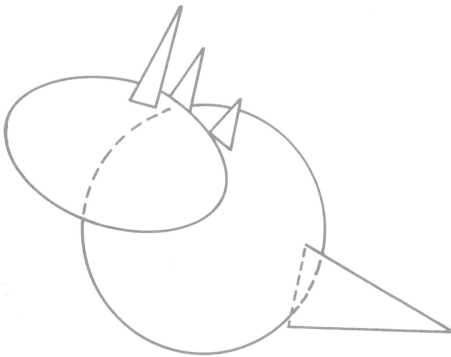

2. Add four legs using ovals and triangles. See how the legs bend where these shapes meet? Then add some small triangles around the back of the head.

3. Using your basic shapes as a guide, create a more realistic shape for *Triceratops*. Erase any extra lines that you don't need.

Hint: Using basic shapes can be helpful even when adding small details, such as toenails. Remember to use guidelines, and if you don't like the way something looks, just erase it and try again.

4. Now put in all the details that will make your *Triceratops* lifelike. Adding toenails, an eye, skin texture, and shading will make it look ready to walk right off your paper!

SPINOSAURUS

(SPY-nuh-SORE-us)

The name, which means "spiny lizard," refers to the long spines on this dinosaur's back.

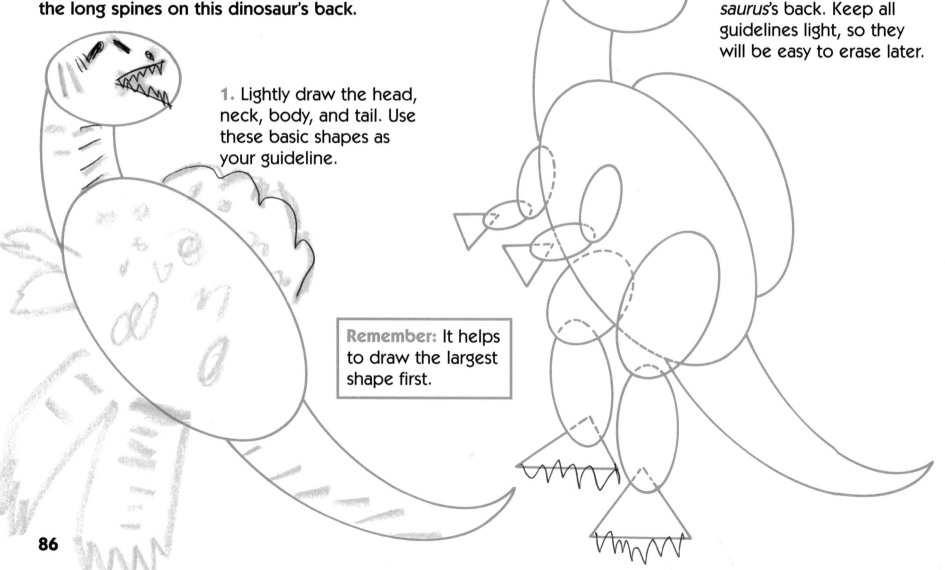

1. Lightly draw the head, neck, body, and tail. Use these basic shapes as your guideline.

2. Add arms, legs, and a guideline for the row of spines on the *Spinosaurus*'s back. Keep all guidelines light, so they will be easy to erase later.

Remember: It helps to draw the largest shape first.

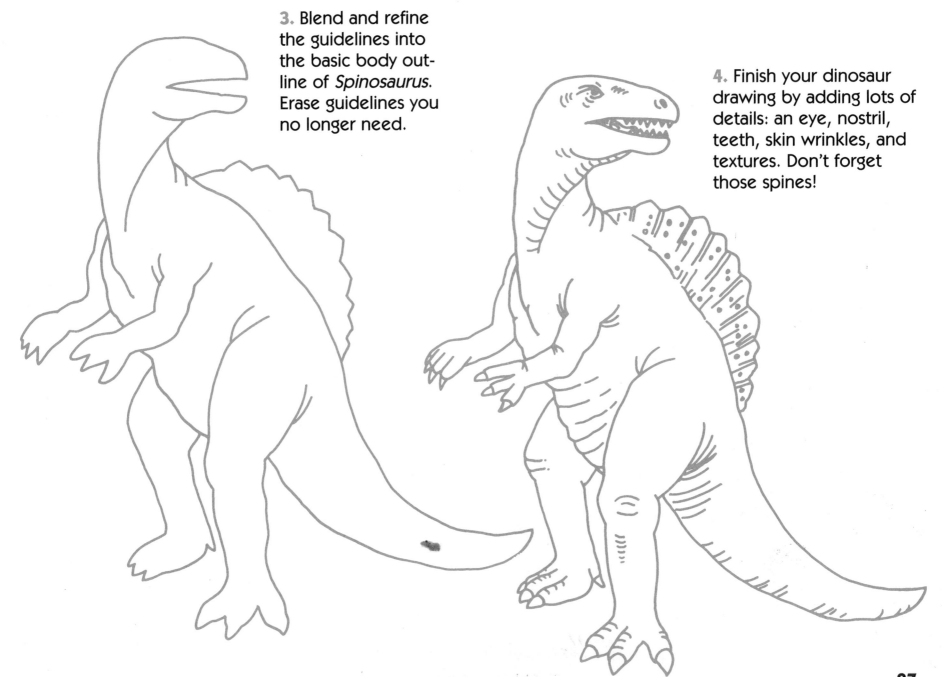

3. Blend and refine the guidelines into the basic body outline of *Spinosaurus*. Erase guidelines you no longer need.

4. Finish your dinosaur drawing by adding lots of details: an eye, nostril, teeth, skin wrinkles, and textures. Don't forget those spines!

TARBOSAURUS

(TAR-boh-SORE-us)

The name means "terrible lizard." This meat-eater's enormous, powerful body and daggerlike teeth must have struck fear into smaller dinosaurs. *Tarbosaurus* is known from 10 complete skeletons found in the Gobi Desert of Mongolia.

2. Add basic shapes for the legs and short arms. Then add a line for the mouth.

1. Lightly sketch three free-form guideline shapes for the body, head, and tail.

3. Add an eye, nostrils, and a tiny hole at the back of the head. Then blend the shapes into a clean outline drawing.

4. Add shading, skin texture, and other details to complete your drawing of terrible *Tarbosaurus*!

Use your imagination to fill this scene with some of the dinosaurs you have learned to draw. Draw some plant-eating dinosaurs as well as meat-eaters.

Hint: Think of scenery as basic shapes, too. Look for ovals, triangles, and free-form shapes as you draw this scene—and others you imagine!

INDEX

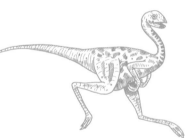

Corythosaurus
page 68

Deinonychus
page 56

Dilophosaurus
page 52

Diplodocus
page 12

Dromaeosaurus
page 72

Hadrosaurus
page 18

Hylaeosaurus
page 54

Ichthyosaur
page 17

Iguanodon
page 22

Lambeosaurus
page 30

Leptoceratops
page 50

Maiasaura
page 66

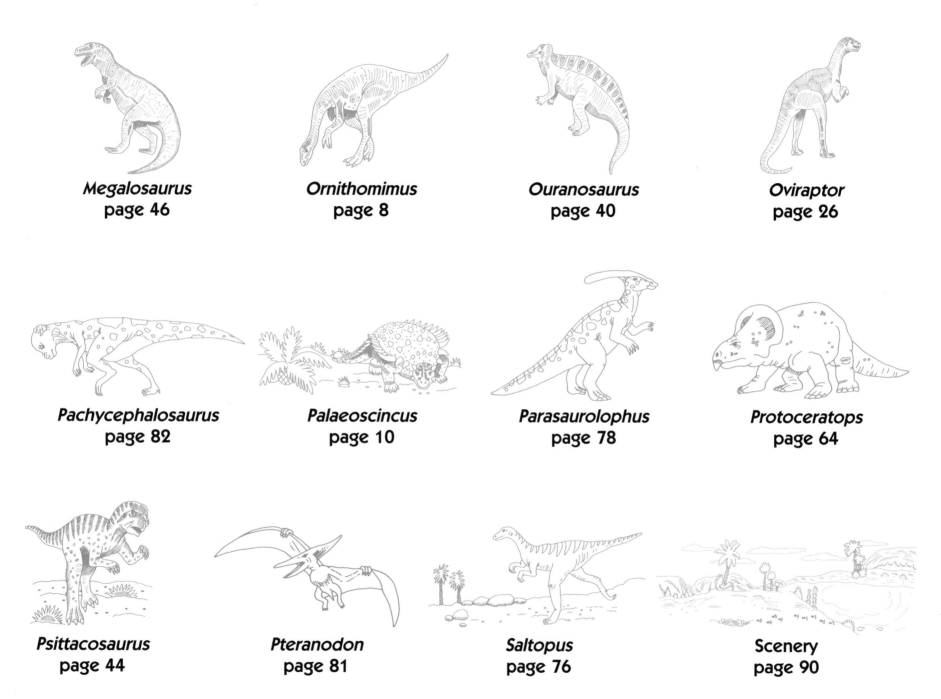

Spinosaurus
page 86

Stegosaurus
page 74

Styracosaurus
page 6

Tarbosaurus
page 88

Triceratops
page 84

Troodon
page 36

Tylosaurus
page 28

Tyrannosaurus
page 70

Velociraptor
page 14